Easy Lawn Care & Maintenance

1st Edition

Contents

Section A: Overview

1. Introduction

If there is one thing recent years have taught us, it is how simple things like being outdoors can make us happy. Fortunately, a garden with lush green grass is achievable for everyone, by following a few basic steps.

This guide will offer simple steps to improve, maintain, and keep your lawn thriving, whether it is the first time you are sowing grass seed or if you are an experienced gardener. We will also go over some additional tips, and insights you can use to resolve common problems and achieve optimal results.

In this section, I offer 5 Quick Steps for sowing grass seed. Followed by a high-level overview of 3 key areas, and finally some information regarding essential and optional equipment related to each stage of lawn maintenance.

2. 5 Quick Steps to Sowing Grass Seed

01 | **BUY HIGH QUALITY GRASS SEED**
- A great lawn can only be grown from great grass seeds.
- A back lawn grass seed mix should be hard-wearing

02 | **PREPARE SOIL**
- Loosen the top 2-3 inches (5-8cm) of soil (New Lawns).
- Mow grass as short as possible (Existing Lawns).
- Remove debris & level areas where excess water collects.
- Apply a starter fertilizer before seeding.
- DO NOT use weed killers before/after sowing.

03 | **SOW GRASS SEED**
- Spread the seed evenly by hand in small areas (35g/sqm or 1oz/sq yd), to cover up to 35m2 (375 ft2).
- Use a hand or lawn spreader for larger areas.

04 | **COVER GRASS SEED**
- Lightly cover the grass seed with topsoil < ¼ inch (0.5cm).

05 | **WATER GRASS SEED**
- Water deeply but don't saturate, and frequently (every 1-2 days) during initial 3-4 weeks.
- Keep grass seed bed moist to enhance germination and growth.

3. High-Level Overview

Sowing grass seed successfully and preparing your lawn can be summarised into three key areas.

Grass Seed

Firstly, buy a high-quality grass seed mixture. Using average seed will never result in the best outcome, no matter how much care you put in. Spend time researching the various lawn seed mixes and reading reviews. Look for the characteristics that matter to you, such as seed that is quick to establish, durable, drought-resistant, and shade-tolerant, among others.

Soil

Secondly, grass seed requires good soil to develop robust roots. Although you may not have ideal soil in your garden, you can certainly improve it. Removing debris, aerating the soil, and using a quality starter fertiliser will significantly improve its condition. Or you can add a thin layer of purchased topsoil – it costs extra but the results are worth it.

Water

Thirdly, grass seed needs water to germinate and grow, especially in the first 3-4 weeks. Watering every 1-2 days during the initial stages will improve the likelihood of successful germination and speed up the germination process. However, if there is rainfall, less watering is required. Water your garden early in the morning or late afternoon when the sun is weak. This helps reduce evaporation and maximise soil absorption. Avoid over-watering as this can lead to standing surface water, which will "drown" the seedlings.

QUICK TAKEAWAYS

1. Use high-quality grass seed mixture for best results.

2. Good soil is essential for grass seed to develop robust roots.

3. Grass seed needs water to germinate and grow, especially in the first 3-4 weeks.

4. Water your garden in the early morning or late afternoon to reduce evaporation and maximise soil absorption.

5. Avoid over-watering, as it can lead to standing surface water and "drown" the seedlings.

4. Equipment

This is the easy overlook of the various essential and optional equipment used in seeding, watering, aerating, raking, rolling, and maintaining of lawn.

1. SEEDING:	
Quality seed mix	Essential
Spreader	Optional

3. WATERING:	
Hosepipe/ sprinkler	Essential
Watering can	Optional

2. AERATING, RAKING & ROLLING	
Garden fork	Essential
Rake	Essential
Aerator	Optional
Roller	Optional

4. MAINTENANCE:	
Lawnmower	Essential
Strimmer	Optional
Wheelbarrow	Optional
Trowel	Optional

Section B: Preparation

5. Preparation & Sowing

This part covers all the essential aspects of preparing and sowing grass seed (including the three different approaches to it). We will also go over the steps involved in preparing a new lawn, over-seeding an existing lawn, and repairing patches of an existing lawn. Additionally, the factors that affect the germination of grass seed and how to improve your chances of success. By the end, you will have a comprehensive understanding of how to create a healthy, beautiful lawn, no matter which approach you choose.

Starting from scratch takes more time and effort, but gives you the opportunity to create a perfect lawn. Sure, it requires more work and effort, and normally costs more than simply over-seeding or rejuvenating an existing lawn.

EASY LAWN CARE & MAINTENANCE

There are broadly three different approaches to sowing grass seed. Your choice will depend on what you are aiming to achieve:

1. Preparing a **new lawn**
2. Improving the condition of an **existing lawn** (over-seeding)
3. Repairing **patches** of an existing lawn

1. Preparing a New Lawn

Starting a new lawn from scratch takes more effort and can be more expensive than simply over-seeding or rejuvenating an existing lawn. But the end result is well worth it. You get the chance to create a high-quality lawn that is tailored to your own personal taste and design.

STEP 1 – REMOVE DEBRIS

- Remove leaves, sticks, rocks, and other loose debris.
- Remove surface weeds and large stones.

STEP 2 – LEVEL THE AREA

- Fill in all the hollows and flatten the bumps.
- Grade & level the soil and site.
- Put down new topsoil if in-situ soil is poor or lacks nutrients.

STEP 3 – REMOVE STANDING WATER

- Drain the site (if required) to ensure there is no standing water.

STEP 4 – AERATE THE SOIL

- Loosen the soil.
- Break down any lumps of soil.

STEP 5 – REMOVE WEEDS

- Remove any weeds (Do Not Use a Weedkiller Within 4-6 Weeks of Sowing).
- Lightly rake the soil.
- Complete final levelling of the surface.

STEP 6 – WATER & FERTILISE THE SOIL

- Lightly water the area being sown with seed.
- Feed the soil with a starter fertiliser.
- Sow the seeds no more than 2-3 days after putting down fertiliser to avoid weed growth.

STEP 7 – SOW THE SEED

- Sow the seed by hand or by using a seed spreader/dropper **(35 grams per m²) or (1 oz/sq yd).**
- If using a spreader, do perpendicular runs.
- Do not put excessive seed down in the same area.
- Protect the seed with string mesh & bird/cage netting (if required).

STEP 8 – WATER THE SEED & GRASS

- Water the soil, seed, and new grass regularly.
- Daily watering during the first 2 weeks is best.
- Less watering is required if there is rainfall.

STEP 9 – CUT GRASS

- Cut & mow the newly germinated grass.
- Take no more than 1/3 off the height.
- Rule of thumb is to do frequent but light cuts.
- Trip the edges.
- Remove all loose cuttings.
- Water the new grass.

2. *Improving the Condition of an Existing Lawn (Over-seeding)*

Over-seeding an existing lawn is a common and effective approach to maintaining a healthy lawn. To ensure your lawn remains in top condition, consider over-seeding it once a season, ideally in April or May. This will boost coverage, improve grass density, and keep your lawn looking its best.

STEP 1 – REMOVE DEBRIS

- Remove leaves, sticks, rocks, and other loose debris.
- Remove surface weeds and large stones.

STEP 2 – LEVEL THE AREA

- Fill in all the hollows and flatten the bumps.
- Put down new topsoil if in-situ soil is poor or lacks nutrients.

STEP 3 – REMOVE STANDING WATER

- Drain the site (if required) to ensure there is no standing water.

STEP 4 – AERATE THE SOIL

- Loosen the soil.
- Break down any lumps of soil.

STEP 5 – REMOVE WEEDS

- Remove any weeds (Do Not Use a Weedkiller Within 4-6 Weeks of Sowing).
- Lightly rake the soil.
- Complete final levelling of the surface.

STEP 6 – WATER & FERTILISE THE SOIL

- Lightly water the area being sown with seed.
- Feed the soil with a starter fertiliser.
- Sow the seeds no more than 2-3 days after putting down fertiliser to avoid weed growth.

STEP 7 – SOW THE SEED

- Sow the seed by hand or by using a seed spreader/dropper **(50 grams per m²) or (1.5 oz/sq yd).**
- If using a spreader, do perpendicular runs.
- Do not put excessive seed down in the same area.

STEP 8 – WATER THE SEED & GRASS

- Water the soil, seed, and new grass regularly.
- Daily watering during the first 2 weeks is best.
- Less watering is required if there is rainfall.

STEP 9 – CUT GRASS

- Cut & mow the newly germinated grass.
- Take no more than 1/3 off the height.
- Rule of thumb is to do frequent but light cuts.
- Trip the edges.
- Remove all loose cuttings.
- Water the new grass.

3. *Repairing Patches of an Existing Lawn*

There are several reasons why grass seed may not germinate optimally (a different mix of sun, temperatures, water, soil, fertiliser, seed density, etc). Frequently, the most likely causes of patches and poor germination are cooler temperatures or frost.

Grass seed requires a minimum of 4 hours direct sunlight a day and temperatures of above 8 degrees Celsius (45 F) for optimal germination. If patches do develop in your lawn, the following steps will help to remove them.

EASY LAWN CARE & MAINTENANCE

STEP 1 – REMOVE DEBRIS

- Remove leaves, sticks, rocks, and other loose debris.
- Remove surface weeds and large stones.

STEP 2 – AERATE THE SOIL

- Loosen the soil or put down new topsoil if in-situ soil is poor or lacks nutrients.
- Break down any lumps of soil and lightly rake the soil.

STEP 3 – WATER & FERTILISE THE SOIL

- Lightly water the patches being sown with seed.
- Feed the soil with a starter fertiliser.
- Sow the seeds no more than 2-3 days after putting down fertiliser to avoid weed growth.

STEP 4 – SOW THE SEED

- Sow the seed by hand or by using a seed spreader/dropper **(35 grams per m²) or (1 oz/sq yd).**
- Do not put excessive seed down in the same area.

STEP 5 – WATER THE SEED & GRASS

- Water the soil, seed, and new grass regularly.
- Daily watering during the first 2 weeks is best.
- Less watering is required if there is rainfall.

There are steps common to all approaches but there are also slight differences. The key points to remember are (a) to loosen the existing soil, (b) use good quality grass seed and (c) water frequently.

KEY TAKEAWAYS
4. Starting a new lawn takes effort and may cost more but offers a chance to create a high-quality lawn tailored to your personal taste.
5. Over-seeding an existing lawn is a common and effective approach to maintaining a healthy lawn. Consider doing it once a season, ideally in April or May.
6. Patches in a lawn may develop due to lack of sunlight and optimal temperature for grass seed germination.
7. To achieve the best results, make sure to loosen the soil, use good quality grass seed, and water frequently.

6. Top Dressing

Top dressing helps replenish soil nutrients, even out dips and hollows, improve soil drainage and water retention, enhance drought resistance, and promote growth of new shoots for a thicker and denser lawn coverage. The ideal time to top dress is early Autumn, around mid-September, after lightly aerating the soil.

Over time nutrients in the soil can become depleted. To keep your lawn healthy and strong, consider adding top dressing every year or every two years at the most. This involves spreading a mixture of topsoil, sand, and humus on the grass. Not only does this help to replenish the soil's nutrients, but it also helps to even out any minor dips or hollows that may have formed over time.

Top dressing your lawn annually, or at least every two years, is crucial in maintaining its health and preventing soil nutrient depletion over time. The ideal time to do this is early Autumn, around mid-September. Before top dressing, it's a good practice to lightly aerate or spike the soil. Then, use the flat back of a rake to evenly spread a mix of topsoil, sand, and humus over the area, making sure that it reaches the base of the grass at soil level and is removed from the grass leaves.

It also improves soil drainage in heavy soils, water retention in sandy soils, and enhances the grass's drought resistance. In addition, it promotes the growth of new shoots which improves the thickness and density of the grass coverage.

KEY TAKEAWAYS

1. Top dressing helps maintain a healthy lawn and prevents soil nutrient depletion.
2. The ideal time for top dressing is early Autumn, around mid-September.
3. Before top dressing, lightly aerate or spike the soil and spread a mix of topsoil, sand, and humus evenly.
4. Top dressing improves soil drainage, water retention, drought resistance, and promotes growth of new shoots, improving grass coverage.

Section C: Maintenance & Management

Now we will go over watering your lawn, lawn feeding, aerating soil, mowing your lawn, and proper lawn care techniques such as rolling, raking and scarifying.

7. Watering

During the first few weeks after sowing grass seed (especially during the first 3-4 weeks), and during periods of low rainfall, water your lawn regularly. The amount, method, and frequency of watering will depend on several factors such as soil condition, time of year, and maturity of the grass.

If your grass turns yellow or brown, it is a sign that it's not getting enough water. A loss of colour in the grass is often noticeable after extended periods of dry weather.

Another risk brought by a lack of water is that weeds such as clover, which are more drought resistant than grass, can gain a foothold and start to grow. To mitigate these risks, you can use the following two methods:

Method 1. Optimal Watering

The amount, method, and frequency of watering are dependent on factors such as the soil condition, time of year, and maturity of the grass. The aim is to replenish the water reserves in the soil, especially during Summer and times of low rainfall.

- For newly sown seeds, water every 1-2 days during the first few weeks (less frequently if it rains).

- For existing grass or a mature garden, water weekly during Spring/Summer and every 10 days during Autumn. During hot, dry weather spells, you should consider watering every 2-3 days.

- If the ground is hard and compact or there is debris covering the grass, it is best to aerate/spike the area (e.g. using a garden fork) and remove any loose debris (e.g., using a garden rake) before watering.

- Use a standard sprinkler or hosepipe for watering (there are many options, but keep it simple).

- For existing grass or a mature garden, it is best to avoid watering the ground lightly or merely dampening the soil, because this does not encourage the formation of deep roots. It is far better to soak the soil to a depth of 2-4 inches (5-10 cm) at a minimum. This roughly translates into 20-30 minutes of watering time when using a standard sprinkler, although it does depend on the soil condition of the area being watered.

Method 2. Improve Resistance to Drought

Increasing the ability of your grass to handle periods of low rainfall is a significant step forward. The aim is to help your grass develop a robust, deep root structure. This can be achieved by taking the following steps:

- Apply a phosphate rich fertiliser on the grass each year

- Try not to cut the grass too short (never more than a 1/3 off the existing height)

- Remove debris and leaves, especially during Autumn

- Lightly aerate and top dress your garden every Autumn

- It is best to soak the soil to a depth of 2-4 inches for 20-30 minutes with a standard sprinkler or hosepipe.

8. Feeding (Compost & Fertiliser)

Whether applying manually or with a spreader, fertilisers help create a lush, thriving lawn with minimal effort. That is because lawn feeding (with compost and fertilisers) provides essential nutrients like Nitrogen, Phosphorus, and Potassium that promote strong growth, resistance to stress and diseases, and vibrant colour in the grass. For best results, it is important to choose the right fertiliser for the right time of year and follow application guidelines such as applying it to moist soil, avoiding rain and watering after application.

While feeding your lawn is not essential, it does help to ensure that the grass has access to the necessary nutrients it requires for healthy growth. The questions to consider are: (1) which fertiliser to use, (2) when to fertilise, and (3) how much fertiliser to use.

Fertilisers are classified by a **NPK ratio,** which represents three important nutrients: Nitrogen (N), Phosphorous (P) and Potassium (K). Each nutrient provides something different to the grass and each one is required at a different time of the year.

NUTRIENT	WHAT IT DOES	WHEN TO APPLY
Nitrogen	Stimulates growth, greens grass	Spring
Phosphorous	Builds robust root structure	Spring/Autumn
Potassium	Develops strength to resist disease & drought	Spring/Autumn

Nitrogen (N)

A fertiliser with a high 'N' value (high in Nitrogen) is generally required in Spring, while it's best to use one with a low 'N' value in Autumn. In Spring look for a ratio of **4**:1:2 or **3**:1:2 (or multiples of this such as 16:4:8) when selecting a fertiliser. If using one in Autumn, choose one with a ratio of **4**:12:12 (or similar).

If the grass starts losing its colour, most common during hot, dry spells in Summer, the grass may also require a small boost of fertiliser to help stimulate growth. Again, a fertiliser rich in Nitrogen is best, such as a **4**:1:2 or BU3:1:2.

Phosphorous (P)

For new grass and newly seeded lawns, grass requires a high level of Phosphorous to help the seedlings develop robust roots. Therefore, the best starter fertilisers are ones with a NPK ratio of 6:**9**:6 or multiples of this such as 12:**18**:12.

⬛ *Potassium (K)*

The final nutrient, Potassium, helps the grass to build up its immunity and resistance against stresses such as drought, heat stress, freezing temperatures, and diseases. It helps strengthen the grass and builds the rigour required to survive weather extremes (freezing Winters and hot Summers).

Application

Before applying a fertiliser, ensure that the soil is moist. However, when applying fertiliser, it should not be raining and the grass should be dry. Lastly, if there has been no rainfall for a couple of days after applying the fertiliser, add water to the soil and area that has been fertilised.

Fertilisers come in both a soluble form and a granular form, but there is no real preference. They can be applied manually or with a spreader. Watering cans or sprayers can be used for soluble fertilisers.

KEY TAKEAWAYS

1. Fertilising your lawn is not mandatory but helps the grass access necessary nutrients.

2. Fertilisers are classified by their NPK ratio, representing Nitrogen (N), Phosphorus (P), and Potassium (K).

3. Nitrogen is the most important nutrient, with a high N value fertiliser required in Spring and a low N value in Autumn.

4. Phosphorus is essential for new grass and seeded lawns, a NPK ratio of 6:9:6 is a suitable starter fertiliser.

5. Potassium strengthens the grass's immunity and helps it survive weather extremes, apply fertiliser when the soil is moist and grass is dry.

9. Aerating

The primary purpose of aerating soil is to make it easier for oxygen and water to penetrate. This encourages growth & root development, improves drainage, and builds drought resistance. Aerating is especially important in Autumn because it allows Winter rainfall to penetrate the soil, which helps avoid moss and thatch build-up on the surface.

The aerating process involves spiking the soil with a simple garden fork or a hollow-tine fork, to relieve compaction and compression.

It is best to push the fork about 5-10 cm (3-5 inches) deep into the soil to break through the compacted top layer.

Areas requiring aeration may exhibit characteristics such as

- Bare batches and a dry/clay-like appearance

- Discolouration and browning of the grass

- Poor drainage and a build-up of water after rainfall

Do not aerate during Spring because the rigour of spiking can damage the roots and new grass blades, as they start to grow around that time.

An alternative is pricking, similar to aerating/spiking but with spikes that only penetrate the soil surface by 3-5 cm (1-2 inches). To perform pricking, you would typically use an aerator tool that has a wheel with spikes on it, which you would push along the ground. The goal is to gently pierce the soil surface and the layer of dead matter on top.

Lastly, it is best to aerate, spike, or prick your lawn after scarifying but before applying any top dressing or overseeding.

10. Rolling, Raking, & Scarifying

Rolling

Rolling should be avoided unless it is necessary to flatten the surface. Rolling will compact the soil and often exaggerates any unevenness on the surface.

It is only necessary in Spring because frost can cause certain areas to raise up. Rolling can help bring the surface back together. Use a roller when the soil is moist and the grass is dry, as this will help the grass 'knit' together more effectively. Just be sure to wait until the soil has had a chance to dry out after any rainfall before using a roller.

Raking

Raking removes any leaves, thatch, and debris that collects on the surface. This restricts the amount of sunlight reaching the blades of grass. That is why raking up grass clippings after mowing is also beneficial. A build-up of debris hampers drainage and can cause surface water to collect. This, in turn can lead to moss forming, especially in Autumn and Winter when conditions are cooler and damper.

Scarifying

Scarifying is the better option when there is a thick build-up of debris or 'thatch' on the surface,. Use a rake with stiffer bristles to effectively break through the thatch and remove debris. But do not use a heavy rake in Spring as it tears up new shoots and blades of grass. It can also lead to a growth in weeds.

Scarifying or heavy raking should not be done until Autumn when it has the most benefit, and the grass is mature and strong.

For **new lawns,** it is worth scarifying and/or raking the area before sowing seeds, irrespective of the time of year. However, as mentioned earlier, do not roll the area being sown because compacting the soil will make it more difficult for the grass seedlings to break through to the surface.

11. Mowing

With mowing, as with everything else, timing, frequency, and cutting height matter a lot.

For a healthy lawn, it's important to follow a few simple guidelines, whether you're mowing a mature lawn or giving your newly seeded lawn its first trim.

When to mow?

Mow between early Spring (March/April) to late Autumn (October/November). It is unwise to mow outside of these periods because it is more important the grass blades retain the nutrients. Try not to mow when the grass is wet or when the soil is overly damp. The rigours of the mower risk pulling the grass blades out at the roots, while the mower itself can damage the softer wet surface.

How often should you mow?

Do frequent but light mows. Typically, cut the grass every 7-10 days during Summer when there is rigorous growth. And every two weeks during Spring and Autumn when the rate of growth slows. Frequent mows encourage the grass to produce tillers or horizontal runners, which increases density and coverage. This builds robustness in the grass and makes it difficult for weeds to take hold. It also adds to the aesthetic appeal of the lawn.

How much to cut?

As a rule of thumb, never cut more than a third off the height of the grass. It should not be cut below 1.5 to 2 inches (4 cm – 5 cm). Grass shorter than this loses nutrients which the roots depend on. Furthermore, the grass is less able to provide insulation from the sun (especially in Summer) and will retain less water.

Conversely, leaving grass to grow too high, above 3.5 to 4 inches (9 cm–10 cm) can also be detrimental to its health. The lower part of the grass blade receives less sunlight and develops less resistance. When the grass is finally cut, the loss of a large portion of the blade shocks the grass, which impacts its health. The lower part of the blade is now more exposed to the elements, and growth is subsequently subdued. The sparse grass cover can also allow weeds to gain a foothold.

Section D: Problems & Challenges

12.   Weeds

Weeds are a persistent problem for both new and established lawns. Weed seeds may stay inactive in the soil until conditions are favourable for germination, so it's important to take preventative measures. If weeds grow, it's important to act quickly.

1. *How to prevent weeds from growing*

You can make it difficult for weeds to germinate in your garden. If you keep your lawn healthy and vigorous, it provides enough competition to prevent weeds from growing and overtaking. If patches of weak or sparse grass develop, weeds will pop up and spread.

Scarifying and Raking

Lightly raking the grass in Autumn removes debris and any thatch that can build up during the Summer. This aids water penetration and allows more sunlight to stimulate grass growth, thereby limiting opportunities for weeds. Do not over-rake or scarify too aggressively, as this will risk thinning out the grass cover.

Watering

Grass requires sufficient water to remain healthy. If your lawn is not well-watered during prolonged hot, dry spells, grass growth will slow, and patches may develop. This results in less competition for weeds dormant in the soil and makes your lawn susceptible to their growth. Therefore, water your lawn during these periods.

Mowing

Sticking to good mowing practices will help ensure that the grass retains the nutrients it needs to stay healthy. It is important not to cut the grass too short and avoid taking off too much during a single cut (aim to remove no more than 1/3 at a time, as a general guideline). Doing frequent, light cuts is always better.

Feeding & Disease Control

Feeding your lawn will stimulate growth and help the grass stay strong. This reduces and removes any bare patches where weeds might start growing. If your lawn is affected by disease, apply the appropriate treatment as soon as possible. If bare patches have developed, re-seed the area with a quality seed mix.

2. *How to Remove Weeds*

If weeds begin to grow, deal with them as soon as possible before they take over. This can either be done by hand (manually) or by applying a treatment (chemically). The preferred method will depend on the quantity and type of weeds growing.

Manual Removal

This method is most suitable when there are only a few weeds. Use a trowel to dig up the weeds or a lawn edger/knife to slice through their centre. Follow this up by raking up the loose weeds and leaves, before mowing. If there are any divots remaining from where the weeds were extracted, fill the with soil and scatter grass seed.

This is the cheaper and preferred method because it does not impact the existing grass and can be applied to almost all weed types. Even though it requires more physical effort, it should be your first consideration.

Chemical Treatment

In cases where weeds are widespread, it's best to apply a weed killer or similar treatment. There are many options available on the market, so do some research or consult with an expert to determine the most appropriate product for the type of weed.

There are some important points and considerations to remember when applying a weed treatment.

> Follow the instructions on the product label or packaging.

> Apply during Summer when growth is at its most rigorous.

> Do not apply during a prolonged dry spell or if rainfall is imminent.

> Do not apply too much at one time because this may scorch the grass.

> Apply when the soil is damp.

> Do not mow the lawn immediately before application.

> Do not sow new grass seed immediately after application (wait 4-6 weeks).

34

3. *New Lawns*

If you're starting a lawn from scratch, it's important to prepare the soil properly. Use a rake or hoe to turn over the soil and remove any weeds that come to the surface. Repeat this process a few times to remove as many weeds and weed seedlings as possible. If you're facing a severe weed issue, it's recommended to use a chemical treatment or weed killer to get rid of the weeds completely.

13. Patches

Variable temperatures and rainfall, heavy usage and traffic, and a lack of maintenance, all have an impact on the condition of our lawns. It is highly likely that at some stage bare patches will occur on your lawn. Nothing to worry about. There are steps you can take to remedy this quickly.

- Try to ascertain the reason for the bare patches e.g. shade, lack of water, lack of nutrients, heavy footfall/traffic, lack of general maintenance, weeds/moss, soil compaction, poor drainage, disease, animals (urine), time of year (frosts) etc.

- If it is due to weeds/moss or disease, apply a treatment to the area and then follow the patch repair steps outlined below.

- If it is poor drainage or compaction, aerate the soil using a garden fork or similar tool and then follow the patch repair steps outlined below.

- If it is due to a lack of maintenance, lack of nutrients, heavy frosts, pet urine or other, then follow the patch repair steps outlined below.

PATCH REPAIR STEPS

- Aerate the soil using a garden fork or similar garden tool.

- Purchase a good quality grass seed and bag of topsoil (optional).

- Lightly spread a fertiliser into the patch and rake the area (optional but recommended if there is a lack of nutrients in the soil).

- Mix the appropriate amount of grass seed into topsoil and spread the soil/seed mix into the patch.

- Alternatively, mix the grass seed directly into the patch itself and cover it with existing topsoil.

- Water the patch twice a day for a week.

- You should see results after 10-14 days.

14. Lawn Diseases

Unfortunately, every lawn can suffer from diseases. Good thing is, these are preventable through basic lawn care and maintenance. If you do not allow the conditions that diseases require, they simply cannot develop.

There are multiple types of diseases, and each one requires a different method of treatment. There are too many to discuss here, so instead, we will highlight several steps you can take to help prevent their development.

1. Water

- Ensure your lawn is well-watered during dry periods so that the grass remains strong.

- The grass should not be wet for extended periods because diseases do well in moist conditions. It is better to water deeply but try not to over-water so that pools of surface water do not remain for lengthy periods.

- Good drainage and topsoil are important.

- Watering in the morning is recommended so that your lawn has time to absorb the water and then dry out in the afternoon sun.

2. Fertiliser

- Apply the correct amount of fertiliser or lawn feed, at the right time of year.

- Too little can starve grass of the nutrients it needs, making it susceptible to diseases.

- Too much fertiliser can weaken roots if the grass grows too quickly. It may also leave too many nutrients in the soil, which then encourages the growth of weeds and a build-up of thatch.

3. Aeration & Raking

- Aerate and top-dress your lawn once a year in Autumn, using the methods previously described.

- Remove any build-up of thatch or debris from the surface, which can create conditions for the development of lawn diseases.

- Scarify and rake any loose material so that the grass receives as much direct sunlight as possible.

4. Mowing

- As a rule of thumb, only cut a third of the height off the grass.

- Cutting too much off will expose and weaken the grass, leaving it vulnerable to disease.

- Do not leave grass to grow too long before cutting it. The shock of mowing grass if it has grown too long, can lead to problems.

- The frequency of mowing is important, it is best to do frequent, light cuts if possible.

5. Pet Urine

- While pet urine is not a disease, it is worth mentioning its impact on your lawn. The truth is that you can do very little to prevent or cure it.

- If it becomes a problem leading to patches or brown areas, the best approach is to apply significant amounts of water.

- If this does not work, you may simply have to re-seed or re-turf the affected areas.

Unfortunately, we do not always have the time to provide this level of lawn care.

Therefore, if you do notice any patches or signs of disease/stress, it is best to take the necessary steps as soon as possible to avoid the problem from getting worse.

KEY TAKEAWAYS

1. Proper Watering: Water your lawn deeply during dry periods but avoid over-watering and keep it from staying wet for extended periods. Water in the morning and make sure there is good drainage and topsoil.

2. Proper Fertilisation: Apply the right amount of fertiliser or lawn feed at the right time of year, avoiding over-fertilisation and under-fertilisation.

3. Aeration and Maintenance: Aerate and top-dress your lawn once a year in Autumn and remove any build-up of thatch or debris, scarifying and raking loose material to allow for direct sunlight.

4. Proper Mowing: Cut only a third of the height of the grass at a time and avoid cutting too much, leading to frequent, light cuts instead of infrequent, drastic cuts.

5. Pet Urine: Pet urine can cause patches or brown areas on your lawn and can be treated by applying significant amounts of water or re-seeding or re-turfing affected areas. Regular lawn care and maintenance can help prevent the development of lawn diseases.

Section E: Soil & Seed Types

15. Soil Types

Topsoil plays an important role in the success and health of your lawn. It provides the nutrients required for growth and helps with drainage and water retention. It also provides a bed for seed germination and root development, and helps oxygen reach the grass roots.

Understanding the characteristics and properties of different soil types will help you determine the best approach for achieving optimal seed germination and grass performance.

There are several different types of soil, each with its own set of characteristics and properties, but the 4 main types are loam, sandy, clay and silt soils.

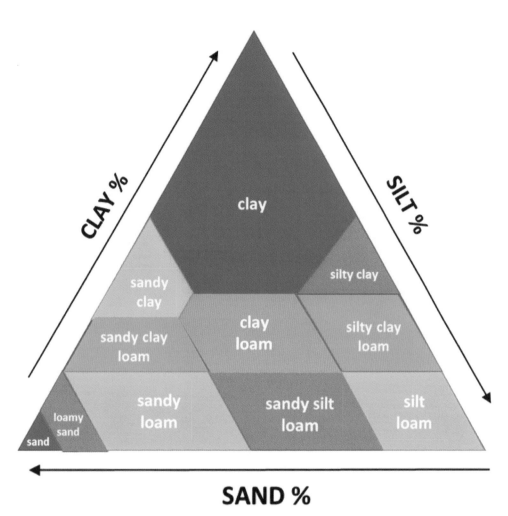

Soil Texture Chart: Sand, Silt and Clay Composition %

A simple, quick test to determine the soil type is to take a handful of damp soil and squeeze it in your hand. Sandy soils will crumble and easily fall apart when you re-open your hand.

For clay soils there will be no cracking and the soil will retain its shape. Clay soils will feel sticky and smooth, whereas sandy soils will feel gritty when you rub it in your hand.

1. Loam Soils

The best type of soil for growing grass is loam soil. It's a mix of sand, silt, and clay, which makes it ideal for growing grass because it holds water well, allowing seed germination, while also providing good drainage after rainfall or watering. Additionally, loam soil is rich in nutrients and allows for good aeration, promoting the development of a strong root system.

2. Sandy Soils

This type of soil runs freely through your hands and doesn't clump together. The biggest challenges with sandy soils are that they have difficulty retaining nutrients and holding water, making it hard for grass to thrive. To address these issues, consider adding compost or other organic, top-dressing materials.

3. Clay Soils

Clay soil is easily mouldable in your hand, and it's packed with nutrients. However, it can be a challenge for grass growth because it retains too much water and doesn't drain well. This can lead to standing water on the surface, which can harm grass seed germination. Plus, the compact soil makes it hard for air to circulate, making it difficult for roots to breathe and for CO_2 to escape. To give your grass a better chance to thrive, consider aerating the soil deeply and adding a top dressing of compost.

4. *Silty Soils*

Silty soils are normally fertile due to their high nutrient content and ability to retain water. However, they are easily compressed and compacted, which makes them difficult to work with. Nevertheless, pure silt soils are very rare in domestic gardens and therefore this soil type does not warrant much attention.

SOIL TYPE	CHARACTERISTICS	TREATMENT
Loam	Average nutrient content	Add organic matter e.g. compost, mulch, manure
	Good drainage	
	Good aeration levels	
	Good water retention	
	Well-balanced (silt, sand, clay)	

SOIL TYPE	CHARACTERISTICS	TREATMENT
Sandy	Low in nutrients	Add organic matter and top dressing e.g. compost.
	Poor water retention	Water thoroughly and regularly during dry periods.
	Drought prone	Add vermiculite and peat.
	Tends to be acidic	Add a slow-relase fertiliser.
	Dry, warm and light-coloured	Water deeply and frequently during dry periods.
Clay	Rich in nutrients	Add organic matter and top dressing e.g. compost.
	Poor drainage	Add gypsum and lime if soil is acidic.
	Compact with low aeration	Improve drainage by raising the surface level.
	Take longer to warm up	Add mulch or manure.
	Sticky and dark coloured	Aerate using a garden fork, aerator or tiller.
Silt	Rich in nutrients (fertile)	Add organic matter e.g. compost, mulch, manure.
	Poor/average drainage	Avoid compacting the soil.
	Good water retention	Add lime or dolomite.
	Easily compacted	Add mulch and manure.
	Very small soil particles	Add a fertiliser.

You will have to balance the time and expense required to prepare and improve the topsoil, with the benefits of optimal seed germination and grass performance. Achieving the best possible topsoil for growing grass is unrealistic and unnecessary in most cases.

KEY TAKEAWAYS

1. Loam soil is the best type of soil for growing grass, as it has a mix of sand, silt, and clay, good water retention and drainage, and rich in nutrients for root development.

2. Sandy soil can be a challenge for grass growth as it has difficulty retaining nutrients and water, but it can be improved by adding compost or other organic top-dressing materials.

3. Clay soil is rich in nutrients, but it can lead to poor grass growth due to its tendency to retain too much water and compact soil, leading to poor aeration and seed germination. Aeration and compost top-dressing can help improve its quality.

4. SilSiltyy soil is fertile and retains water well, but it can be easily compacted, making it difficult to work with, and it is not common in domestic gardens.

5. Balancing the cost and effort of soil preparation with the benefits of optimal seed germination and grass performance is important in achieving the best possible topsoil for growing grass.

16.   Seed Varieties

There are various grass seed varieties available, and each has its own growth habits, unique features and characteristics. Typically grass seed mixes include several different species or varieties. Therefore, it is best to select a grass seed mix with varieties that best meet your requirements. The table shows a list of common grass seed species and their characteristics.

	Perennial Ryegrass	Chewings Fescue	Creeping Red Fescue	Bent
Cold Tolerance	V Low	Low	Low	Medium
Disease Tolerance	High	Medium	Medium	Low
Drought Resistance	Medium	High	High	Medium
Fast-Growing	V High	Low	Medium	Low
Hard Wearing	V High	Low	Medium	Low
Heat Tolerance	V Low	Medium	Medium	High
Nutrients	V High	Low	Medium	Medium
Shade Tolerance	Medium	Medium	Medium	Medium
Thickness/Density	Low	V High	High	V High
Colour	High	Low	Low	V High

Common Grass Seed Varieties Chart: Key Characteristics

1. Ryegrass Varieties

Ryegrass is the most common type of grass seed used in the UK. It is a hard-wearing and fast-growing variety which is why it is included in the majority of amenity and residential lawn mixes. Technically it is a 'bunch grass' or cool-season grass that thrives in most soil types and conditions.

Ryegrass produces a coarse leaf and grows prostrate. This helps it to suppress weed growth. The hardiness and versatility of ryegrass also mean it requires less ongoing maintenance, which is an attractive feature to many people.

2. Fescue Varieties

Fescue is a thin blade of grass that creates a thicker look and is softer beneath your feet. Its fine leaves produce good coverage through dense growth, notably creeping red fescue and its creeping growth habit.

Fescue has a high shade tolerance and is known for its drought resistance. Unlike most other grass seed varieties, it grows well in sunny, shady, and cold conditions. The main downside is that it normally requires slightly warmer soil temperatures to germinate and therefore grows less well if it is sown in cooler months.

3. Bent Varieties

Bent is a fine ornamental grass with leaves that are a rich, green colour. It is a relatively short grass variety and fills in the base, which can be mown very short for a beautiful velvety lawn.

Comparatively it is rather high-maintenance grass, which is why it's usually mixed with fescue to make the lawn hard-wearing and versatile. Nevertheless, aesthetically its richly coloured leaves soften the overall look of your lawn and give it a lush, green appearance.

Type of Growth

The above grass seed varieties do not grow by creating rhizomes. Instead, their "spreading growth" habit is due to grass tiller activity, which is induced through mowing. Rhizomes are the main stem that runs underground horizontally and allow new shoots to grow upwards. Rhizomes are associated with clovers, other legumes, and weeds such as couch.

KEY TAKEAWAYS

1. Ryegrass is a popular grass seed variety in the UK due to its hardiness, fast growth, and low maintenance requirements.

2. Fescue has a high shade tolerance, drought resistance, and can grow well in various conditions. However, it requires warmer soil temperatures to germinate.

3. Bent is a fine ornamental grass that is short and gives a lush, green appearance to the lawn but is high maintenance.

4. The growth of the mentioned grass seed varieties is not through rhizomes, but due to grass tiller activity induced through mowing.

5. When selecting grass seed mix, choose a mix with varieties that best meet your requirements based on the specific characteristics and traits of each species.

Section F: Conclusion

17.   Conclusion

There is a unique pleasure in sowing grass seed, and seeing it grow into dense, lush, green grass – a soft lawn to enjoy and relax on.

Just follow a few simple steps and use the lawn care calendar below. Whether you are establishing a new lawn, overseeding an existing one, or filling in patches, it can be extremely rewarding when you see your grass growing well and your lawn looking healthy.

We hope this short guide has provided some clear and easy-to-follow instructions for improving your lawn. In it we have discussed the steps you can take and offered some tips and insights, to achieve best results. Suitable for both the complete novice and seasoned gardener, our aim has been to make this book helpful and insightful to all.

18. Lawn Care Calendar

MONTH	ACTIVITY
January	Remove leaves and other debris from the grass.
February	"Do not start mowing during February. If weather allows it, start preparing soil at the end of the month."
March	"Remove leaves and other debris from the grass. Do first cut, keep light and do not take too much off the height. Apply moss treatment if required. Prepare soil and sow new seed if creating a new lawn (weather dependent)."
April	"Sow grass seed for new lawns if not done in March. Apply weed treatment if required. Put down fertilizer and lawn feed. Fill in any patches and gaps with soil and grass seed mix."
May	"Increase mowing frequency and do slightly lower cuts. Water grass during dry spells."
June	"Mow grass frequently (weekly). Apply lawn feed (nitrogen based) if required. Remove any weeds that have survived the weed treatment in April."
July	"Continue with frequent mowing. Water grass during dry, hot periods. Apply weed and/or lawn feed treatments if required."

MONTH	ACTIVITY
August	"Continue with frequent mowing. Water grass during dry, hot periods. Apply weed and/or lawn feed treatments if required."
September	"Reduce frequency of mowing and raise cutting height. Apply autumn fertiliser and lawn feed. Scarify, spike and apply top dressing. Repair any patches with soil and seed mix. Apply disease treatments if there is evidence of diseases. Prepare soil and sow seeds if creating a new lawn."
October	"Reduce frequency of mowing and raise cutting height. Apply autumn fertiliser and lawn feed. Scarify, spike and apply top dressing. Repair any patches with soil and seed mix. Water seeds sowed in September."
November	Only mow at beginning of the month and ensure it is a high cut.
December	Remove leaves and other debris from the grass.

19.   Acknowledgements

Hessayon, D.G. (2014). The lawn expert. London: Expert Books.

Mellor, D. (2003). The Lawn Bible. Hyperion.

Akeroyd, S. (2019) Perfect lawns. London: National Trust.

Printed in Great Britain
by Amazon